YEGA ORUTOORO

Learn Rutooro Language

Julian Businge
Tracy Guma

Greatness University Publishers
info@greatness-university.com
www.greatness-university.com

ISBN: 978-1-913164-89-8
ISBN-13: 978-1-913164-89-8

DEDICATION

This book is dedicated to you because you have the passion of learning and speaking Rutooro. Thank you for investing in this book. Thank you for investing in yourself. Thank you for investing in your future. May the knowledge in this book help you to increase your love for Tooro, its customs and culture.

DISCLAIMER

Whilst all attempts have been made to verify the information provided in this book, the authors do not assume any responsibility for errors, omissions or contrary interpretations of the subject matter contained therein. The information provided in this book is for educational and entertainment purposes only.

CONTENTS

Acknowledgements

All praise, honour and glory to our Lord Jesus Christ for the richest grace, mercy and guidance to accomplish this book. In preparation of "Yega Orutooro", we have had help and guidance from some of the most respected people, who deserve our deepest gratitude.

As the completion of this goal gave us much pleasure, we would like to thank, the King of Tooro, His Royal Highness Dr Oyo Nyimba Kabamba Iguru Rukidi IV, Mr. Joe Atwoki Birungi, Mr. Guma Komwiswa, Dr Patrick Businge on behalf of Greatness University Publishers for giving us assistance to the birth of this book, Mr. Kabenge Misisera and Tricia Nyamata, who gave our ideas meaning. You are all a special blessing to us and your passion for the development of the Rutooro language has a lasting effect on us all.

We would also like to extend our gratitude to all those who have directly and indirectly guided us in writing this book. To our dear friends, relatives and in-laws, who have made valuable comments and suggestions; your input has inspired us and immensely contributed to the publication of "Yega Orutooro".

Our dearest families, especially our children, thank you for your extended moral and emotional support during the compilation of this book.

God bless you all.

Foreword

His Majesty Oyo Nyimba Kabamba Iguru Rukidi IV, The King of Tooro Kingdom

Foreword

It gives me great pleasure to introduce to you, "Yega Orutooro" (Learn the Rutooro Language). Rutooro Language is a heritage and identity of the People of the Kingdom of Tooro located in South Western Uganda.

Rutooro is the principal glue that binds us as a distinct group of people. It is a means of communication. It reflects and shapes our values, beliefs and aspirations as Batooro people. It is through Rutooro that we transmit our experiences, our traditions and our knowledge from generation to generation. Cultural heritage is the legacy of tangible and intangible culture and natural heritage which is inherited from past generations, maintained in the present and bestowed for the benefit of future generations.

However, in the face of globalisation and a changing world, Orutooro is increasingly threatened with disappearing and taking with it our entire cultural and intellectual heritage. It is therefore pertinent and imperative that we celebrate, promote and preserve our language, Rutooro for the present and future generations.

The best way to celebrate, promote and preserve our cultural heritage and Rutooro language is to share it with others. I therefore, commend Tracy Guma Adyeri and Julian Businge Amooti for their admirable effort and work in preparing and publishing "Yega Orutooro" which will promote and help preserve the Rutooro language.

I call upon every Mutooro to be proud of our heritage, ancestral roots and identity and to become the Custodians and Guardians of our language, Rutooro. I urge you to promote and preserve Rutooro by learning, teaching and speaking Rutooro with your children and ensuring that you safeguard and pass our precious language, Rutooro and our cultural heritage and identity from our generation to the next.

I invite you all to read and share "Yega Orutooro". Thank you.

**Oyo Nyimba Kabamba Iguru Rukidi IV
King of Tooro Kingdom in Uganda**

Julian Businge & Tracy Guma

Introduction

As parents bringing up children in the diaspora, we have realised the importance of teaching our children their cultural attributes, customs and heritage. It quickly became apparent to us that the best way to do this was through language. It is our responsibility to encourage learning in our children to preserve our rich heritage and the Rutooro language. By breaking the language barrier and universal codes of communication such as the alphabet, numbers, colours and shared values across the world, anybody can therefore learn not just Rutooro but any other language.

Rutooro is spoken by the people of Tooro in South Western Uganda. The people of Tooro are known as the Batooro, with a very rich culture heavily reliant on tribal customs and are people of very high self-esteem.

People learn new languages for various reasons such as work commitments, travel and tourism, intermarriages or an individual challenge to better understand other cultures thus broadening perspectives. This book sets out to assist anyone who wants to learn and or expand on their spoken and written Rutooro. We also hope that this book is helpful to our readers during their travels and Batooro children living in the diaspora or different cities in Uganda, where they are not exposed to the language as often.

Pronunciations and spellings in Rutooro are constantly challenged and often debatable by many, but we welcome your suggestions and corrections for future publications. As a result, this book is not only for beginners or speakers at intermediate level but also for exceptional speakers and readers who can contribute towards developing, capturing and sharing Tooro culture and the Rutooro language to a wider audience. The challenges of learning and mastering a new language are many however, do not be discouraged by this. It will all be worth it when you visit the geographically blessed land of Tooro or share and teach this rich language to your friends and family wherever you are in the world.

Tooro is blessed with golden grasslands, luscious green vegetation, spectacular scenery, good climate and a tranquil environment. We encourage our readers to visit Tooro, the land of beauty and enjoy some of these great attributes, but to also use this opportunity to improve your grammar and build on your vocabulary.

Yega Orutooro

Greetings

Kuramukya

Greetings
Kuramukya

English	Rutooro	Responses
Good Morning	Oraire Ota	Ndaire kurungi (I slept well)
Good Afternoon	Osibire Ota	Nsibire kurungi (I am well)
Good Evening	Oirirwe Ota	Nyirirwe kurungi (I am well)
Good Night	Orale Kurungi	Naiwe Orale kurungi (Good night too)

Greeting Phrases

Welcoming people to your home
Kutangirra abagenyi muka yawe

Welcome visitor

Kaije Mugenyi

Welcome visitors

Kaije Bagenyi

Lovely to find you home

Kasangwe

Hello, what is your name?

Ibara lyawe niiwe oha?

I am called Rose. What is yours?

Ninyowe Rose, Kandi iwe?

I am called Jane

Ninyowe Jane

How are you Rose

Oliy ota Rose

I am fine thank you

Ndi kurungi

Nice to meet you Jane

Nsemerirwe kukurora Jane

Good bye

Ogorobe

I must say goodbye

Kangende caali

Safe journey

Ogende kurungi

May God keep you

Ruhanga akulinde

Pet Names
Empaako

Empaako are used in Tooro instead of a first name to express fondness or familiarity. Each Empaako has a meaning that implies high praise or respect to someone else. When addressing their parents, children always use empaako. Friends address each other using empaako. No one ever chooses one's own empaako; all are assigned by respected elders of the community.

Pet Names Commonly used by Females

- Atwoki means bride or bridegroom
- Amooti means royalty
- Akiiki means saviour of nations
- Adyeri means happy and friendly
- Abwoli means catlike

Pet names for Male Only

- Acaali for chiefs
- Apuuli doglike,
- Araali   means like thunder]
- Abbala
- Okaali for the Omukama/King only

Pet names for both male and female

- Abbooki
- Atwooki
- Ateenyi
- Amooti
- Akiiki
- Adyeri

Greeting in Tooro

If you don't know the pet name of the person you want to greet, you ask them:

Empaako yawe?

> **What is your pet name?**

Eyange Amooti

> **Mine is Amooti**

Empaako yange niyo Apuuli.

> **My pet name is Apuuli.**

Ninyowe Apuuli.

> **I am Apuuli.**

Ota Apuuli?

> **How are you Apuuli?**

Ndi Kurungi Apuuli, iwe oliyota?

> **I am fine Apuuli, how are you?**

Kurungi

> **I am fine.**

Gender

Obuhangwa

Gender	Obuhangwa
Male	Kisaija
Female	Kikazi
People	Abantu
Man	Musaija
Woman	Mukazi
Girl	Mwisiki
Baby	Nkerembe
Child	Mwana
Old man	Mugurusi
Old woman	Mukaikuru
Old boy	Mwojo

Relationship
Obuzaale

First Person: My	
Father	Taata, Ise nyowe
Mother	Mama/ Nau, Nyina nyowe
Mummy	Mama
Sister	Wamau, Wa nyinanyowe
Brother	Wamau, Wa nyinanyowe
Paternal Uncle	Tatento, Isento nyowe
Maternal Uncle	Marumi, Nyinarumi nyowe
Paternal Aunt	Katenkazi
Maternal Aunt	Mawento
Grandmother	Mukaaka
Grand Father	Tatenkuru
Maternal Cousin	Wa mawento
Paternal Cousin	Wa tatento
Nephew	Mwihwa wange

Second Person: Your	
Father	Iso, Taata wawe
Mother	Nyoko, Mama wawe
Mummy	Mama wawe
Sister	Wanyoko
Brother	Wanyoko
Paternal Uncle	Swento
Maternal Uncle	Nyokoromi
Paternal Aunt	Swenkati
Maternal Aunt	Nyokwento
Grandmother	Nyokwenkuru
Grand Father	Swenkuru
Maternal Cousin	Wa nyokwento
Paternal Cousin	Wa swento
Nephew	Mwihwa wawe

Third Person: His/ Hers

Father	Ise
Mother	Nyina
Mummy	Mamawe
Sister	Wanyina
Brother	Wanyina
Paternal Uncle	Isento
Maternal Uncle	Nyinarumi
Paternal Aunt	Isenkati
Maternal Aunt	Nyinento
Grandmother	Nyinenkuru
Grand Father	Isenkuru
Maternal Cousin	Wa nyinento
Paternal Cousin	Wa isento
Nephew	Mwihwawe
Niece	See notes below

Notes:

In Batooro culture :

Cousin only applies between kids whose fathers are brothers or whose mothers are sisters. In both cases they are regarded as sisters or brothers. The above words are more descriptive.

Children refer to paternal uncles as "young/subsidiary dad/mom" even when the uncle/aunt is older than the father.

Nephew or niece (omwihwa) only refers to the relationship between a man and kids of his sisters – not brothers.

A man's brothers' kids are addressed as his sons or daughters. A woman's sisters' kids are addressed as her sons or daughters.

Traditionally a Mutooro woman refers to the kids of her brothers as daughters or sons and does not refer to them as nephews/nieces – abaihwa. The reason being; my sister and my kids are of the same clan whereas my sister's kids belong to another clan.

Questioning

Kukaguza

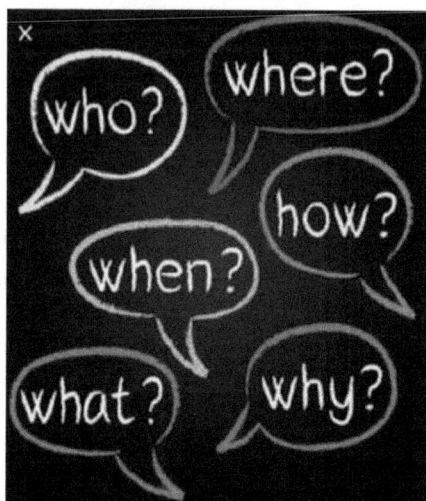

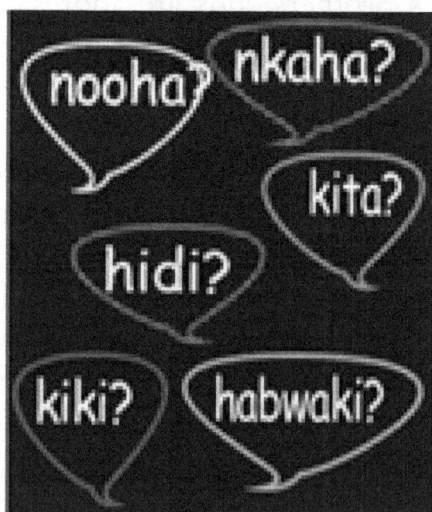

Kaguza ebikaguzo

Nkaha?	Where?
Nogenda nkaha? Nogya nkaha?	Where are you going?
Noruga nkaha? Noruga ha?	Where are you coming from?
Kiki?	What?
Kiha	Which?
Nokora ki?	What are you doing?
Noseka ki?	What are you laughing at?

Now ask the question 'Ogu nooha?' before giving the answer. For example, Ogu Nooha? Mukuru Wisomero.

Ogu nooha?   Who is that?

ANSWER

Mukuru Wisomero	Headmaster
Musomesa	Teacher
Mugenyi	Visitor
Muzaire	Parent
Mugabi watikiti	Conductor
Mu poliisi	Policeman
Musubuzi	Merchant
Mubazizi w'engoye	Tailor
Mugorozi w'engoye woman	Laundry

Conversations About Health

Nozoka ojwahire Orwaire?	You look tired. Are you ill?
Ningira nkwasirwe ekihinzi	I think I have a cold
Nomanyiraha?	How do you know?
Omumiro nigunsarra	My throat is sore

Julian Businge & Tracy Guma

Tooro Kingdom

The Flag of Tooro Kingdom

Ebendera y'Obukama bwa Tooro

The Court of Arms in Tooro Flag

Tooro Kingdom

Akororraho akali mubendera

Yega Orutooro

The King of Tooro

Omukama Wa Tooro

Our King is
Oyo Nyimba Kabamba- Iguru Rukidi

Omukama waitu nuwe
Oyo Nyimba Kabamba- Iguru Rukidi

The Queen Mother is
Best Olimi Kemigisa

Nyina Omukama nuwe
Best Olimi Kemigisa

The Princess Royal is
Ruth Nsemere Komuntale

Batebe nuwe
Ruth Nsemere Komuntale

Ekikaali ky'Omukama

The King's Palace

Tooro Kingdom Anthem

Verse 1
Agutamba Omukama Waitu,
Omukama Entale Ya Tooro,
Karamale Omukuma Nfuuzi,
Hangiriza Mwebingwa

Chorus
Omukama Waitu Murungi,
Omukama Emanzi Ya Tooro,
Karamale Omukuma Nfuuzi,
Hangiriza Mwebingwa

Verse 2
Okulema Kwawe Kurungi
Abanaku Obakwatirra,
Abahabire Obahabura,
Kituli Kinobera Abeemi.

Verse 3
Asingire Omwisa Kihika,
Narolerra Itweena Abantu Be,
Natutegekera Ebirungi,
Hakyaro Nyamunyaka.

Verse 4
Lerunu Itwena Abantu Be,
Banyoro Hamu Nabatungwa,
Tumugonze Tumuhurrege,
Atulemege Nobusinge

Message in the Tooro Kingdom Anthem

TOORO KINGDOM

The Tooro Anthem is song of praise, devotion and patriotism. Here is a general message contained in this anthem.

Our King is the Lion of Tooro. Long live our King. His reign is great.

He helps the poor, directs the lost and plans for his people while sited majestically on the throne.

Us his people, men and women should love and listen to him so that he reigns in peace.

Royal Vocabulary

Here are some of the words used when talking with or about the King of Tooro

English	Rutooro	Royal Rutooro
Good morning	Oraire ota	Zona Okali
Good afternoon	Osibire ota	Hangiriza Okali
Good evening	Oirirwe ota	Gorobya Okali
To bathe	Kunaaba	Kugya hamunabo
To come	Kwija	Kuboneka Kuzooka
To die	Kufwa	Kutuuza
To dress up	Kujwara	Kujwaza
To drink alcohol	Kunywa amaarwa	Kuboneka empotole
To drink milk	Kunywa Amata	Kusingisa
Be buried	Kuzikwa	Kutabazibwa
To get drunk	Kutamira	Kusaijahara
To be	Kujumbira	Kunaga

engaged		orukwanzi
To get sick	Kurwara	Kusasa
To go	Kugenda	Kusimbuka ebyemo
To go and dine	Kugenda kulya	Kugenda haruhango
To have a haircut	Kumwa isoke	Kurabyamu
To laugh	Kuseka	Kwera
To leave	Kuturuka	Kukubya
To leave a throne	Kwimuka ha ntebe	Kugorroka
To dress	Kujwara abijwaro	Kutoza engaju
To sit	Kwikarra ha mulyango	Kusinga hamusanga
To sleep	Kubyaama	Kuraihya/ Kutemba
To stand	Kwemerra	Kusimba omubyemo
To undress	Kujuura	Kujuza
To wake up	Kwimuka	Kuhasuka
Bathroom	Eryogero	Eryambuko
Bed	Ekitabu	Ekihango
Grave	Ekituuro	Egasani

Julian Businge & Tracy Guma

Cultural Heritage Items

Ebintu By'obuhangwa

Yega Orutooro

These are special items used during ceremonies in Tooro and they preserve the cultural heritage. Most of the items are fashioned and designed by the Batooro.

Icumu 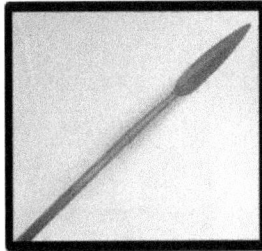 **Spear**

Ekiibo  **Basket**

Engoma  **Drum**

Ensoha  Pot

Ekyanzi  Milk pot

Omukeeka  Mat

Yega Orutooro

Ekanzu		Male cultural tunic

Esuuka		Female cultural wear

Enkeeto		Skin
Omuguta		Hide

Totems and Clans

Omuziro gwange engabi.
My totem is the kob.
Which clan am I?
Mubiito

Omuziro gwange enjojo
My totem is the elephant.
Which clan am I?
Mwiruntu

Omuziro gwange enkende.
My totem is the vervet
monkey.
Which clan am I?
Muhinda

Omuziro gwange embogo.
My totem is the buffalo.
Which clan am I?
Mufumambogo

Abachwezi **Omuziro gwange obusito**
My totem is obusito
(pregnant cow).

Abayanja **Omuziro gwange ente kitale.**
My totem is kitale (white
cow).

Abasiita **Omuziro gwange muka**
My totem is muka
(dew on grass).

Julian Businge & Tracy Guma

Houses

Ebika by'enju

Yega Orutooro

Enju
y'obunyasi

Thatched
house

Gorofa

Flat

Mwamba

Bungalow

Orwigi

Door

Orusu

Roof

Idirisa

Amadirisa

Window

Windows

Yega Orutooro

Esaaha   Clock

Ebalaza   Veranda

Amasanyarazi   Electricity

Amabate — Iron sheets

Kufuru — Locks

Erangi — Paint

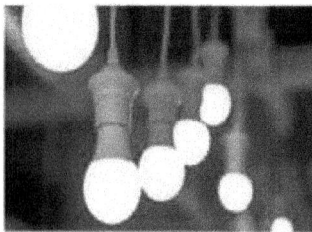

Amataara — Lights

Yega Orutooro

Orugo — Fence

Ekisagate — Wall Fence

Ezigati — Compound

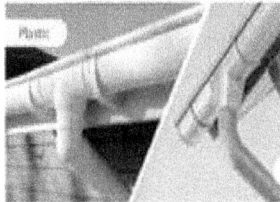

Emigongo — Gutters

Julian Businge & Tracy Guma

Kitchen

Ekicumbiro

Yega Orutooro

Kitchen Utensils

Ebintu eby'omukicumbiro

Ebigiiko	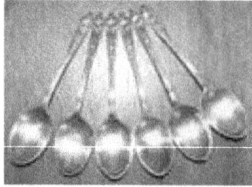	Spoons
Omuhyo	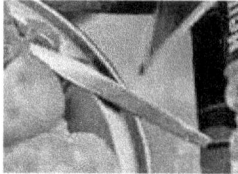	Knife
Omurro	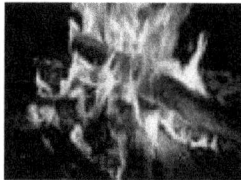	Fire
Ekibiriiti		Matchbox

Yega Orutooro

Enku      Firewood

Esahani      Plates

Ewuma      Forks

Omwiko      Stick

Sukali 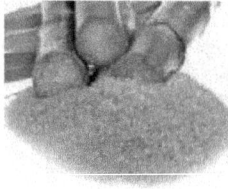 Sugar

Ekikopo  Cup

Gilasi  Glass

Ekipira  Jerrycan

Safuliya  Pan

Kabada  Cupboard

Ebinika  Kettle

Ebuuli  Jug

Furampeni

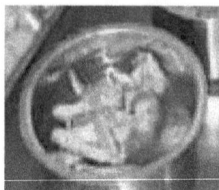

Frying Pan

Ensoha

Pot

Ebyokulya

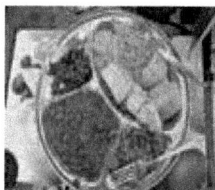

Food

Obuhoro

Leftover food

Yega Orutooro

Bathroom

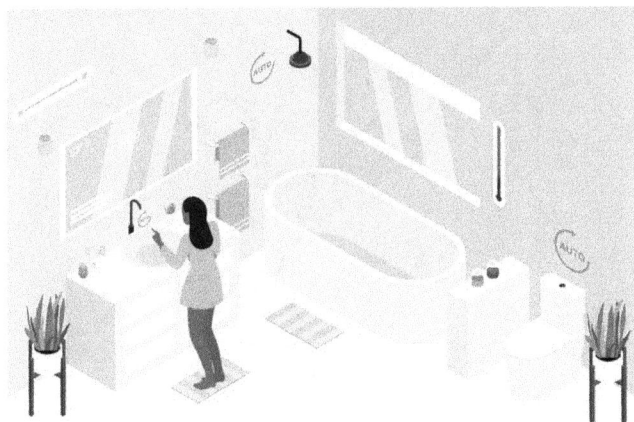

Ekinabiro

Julian Businge & Tracy Guma

Bathroom Utensils

Eby'omukinabiro

Yega Orutooro

Ebafu  Basin

Amaizi  Water

Esabuni 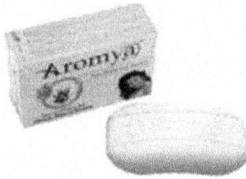 Soap

Ekijum-
ankuba  Sponge

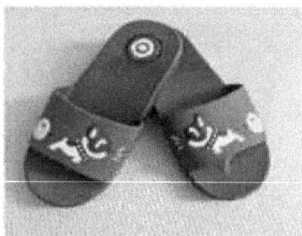

Silipa — Slippers

Enkaito — Shoes

Tawulo — Towel

Ekinazi — Toilet

Yega Orutooro

Bedroom

Ekisiika

Ekitabu  Bed

Omufaliso  Mattress

Amasuuka 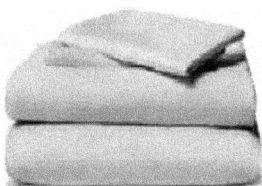 Bedsheets

Blangiti  Blanket

Yega Orutooro

Kabada — Wardrobe

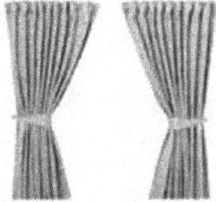

Entimbi — Curtains

Pasi — Flat iron

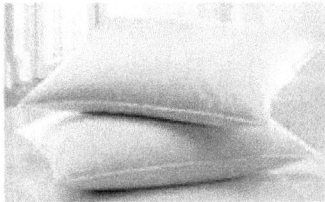

Akasago — Pillow

Food

Ebyokulya

Ebicooli   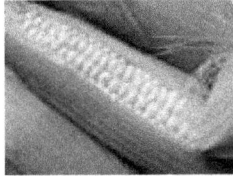   Maize

Ebilaaya      Irish potatoes

Ebitakuli      Sweet potatoes

Ebitooke  Bananas

Muhogo  Cassava

Oburo 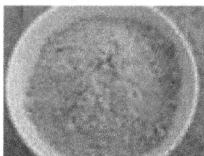 Millet

Omuceeri 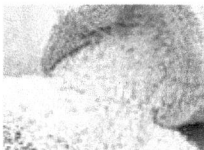 Rice

Omugusa  Sorghum

Yega Orutooro

Omwongo  Pumpkin

Amahuuli  Eggs

Ebihimba  Beans

Ebinyobwa 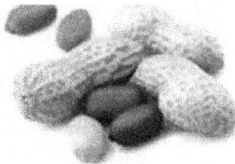 Peanuts

Enjagi  Egg plants

Enkoko 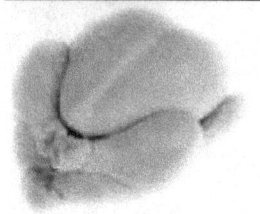 Chicken

Enyama 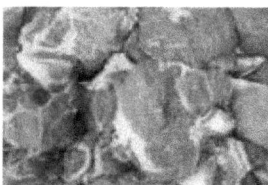 Meat

Enyanya  Tomatoes

Obutunguru  Onions

Yega Orutooro

Drinks

Ebyokunywa

Drinking water	Amaizi gokunywa
Tea with milk	Chai y'amata
Black tea	Chai mukaro
Coffee	Kaawa
Porridge	Obuseera
Juice	Ensande
Banana juice	Ensande y'ebitooke
Beer	Amaarwa
Wine	Eviini
Broth/ Soup	Omucuuzi

Yega Orutooro

Fruits

Ebijuma

Omucunguwa

Orange

Enazi

Coconut

Ipeera

Guava

Ipapaali

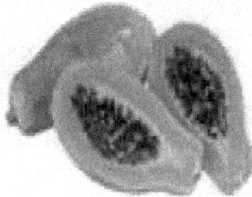

Pawpaw

Omuyembe  Mango

Fene 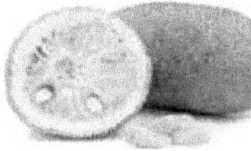 Jack
fruit

Entuutu  Goose
berries

Vakedo  Avocado

Ebyenju

Ripe
bananas

Water
melon

Water
melon

Enanasi

Pineapple

Obusukaali

Sweet
bananas

Endimo		Lemon
Ekikaka		Sugar cane
Kokowa		Cocoa
Mustaferi		Soursop
Obutunda		Passion fruits

Common Expressions

Mum is squeezing oranges.
Mama najunga emicunguwa.

Tooro's avocado is sweet.
Vakedo za Tooro nizinura.

The child is eating.
Omwana naalya.

Cocoa is grown in Bundibugyo.
Kokowa erimwa Bundibugyo.

Muheho ekikaka.
Give him some sugarcane.

Go to the market and buy jack fruit.
Genda omukatale ogule fene.

Yega Orutooro

Hotel Menu

Menu ya Hoteri

Oburo  Millet meal

Omugati  Bread

Ebijuma  Fruits

Amahuli  Eggs

Yega Orutooro

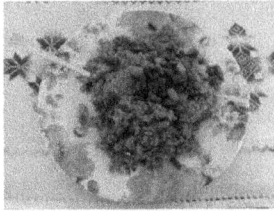

Omuceeri   Rice

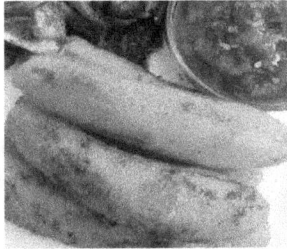

Ebitooke   Bananas

CONVERSATION IN A RESTAURANT

What type of food do you want to eat sir?
N'ogonza kulya ebyokulyaki waitu?

Yes sir, what do you have, what is there?
Ego waitu, mwineyoki, harohoki?

We have eggs, fruits, matooke, rice, millet bread, fish and bread.
Twine Amahuli, ebijuma, ebitooke, omuceri, oburo,ebyenyanja n'omugaati.

77

Grammar

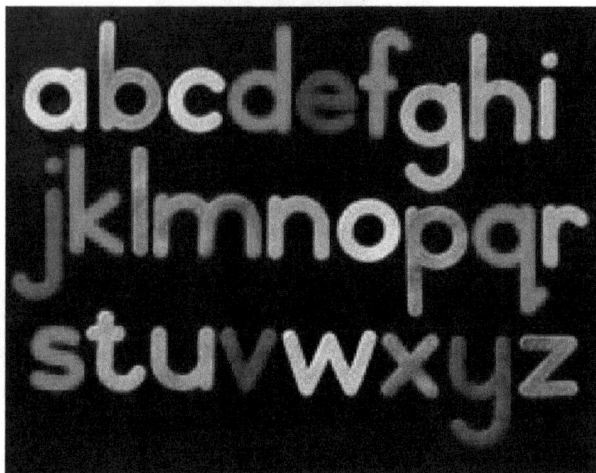

Words that give meaning
Ebigambo Ebiha Amakuru

To see	-	Kurora
To bathe	-	Kwoga
To eat	-	Kulya
To Pray	-	Kusaba
To go	-	Kugenda
To sit	-	Kwikaarra
To play	-	Kuzaana
To stand	-	Kwemeerra
To jump	-	Kuguruka
To clean	-	Kusemeza
To run	-	Kwiruka
To sleep	-	Kubyama
To walk	-	Kurubata
To dance	-	Kwecanga
To write	-	Kuhandiika
To beat	-	Kuteera
To sing	-	Kuzina
To wash	-	Kunaaba (for people)
To wash	-	Kwogya (for clothes)
To teach	-	Kwegesa
To buy	-	Kugura

Pronouns

Pronoun English	Pronoun Rutooro	Present auxiliary	Past auxiliary	Future
I	Nyowe	Nin	Nka	Ndi
We	Itwe	Nitu	Tuka	Tuli
You Singular	Iwe	No	Oka	Oli
You Plural	Inywe	Nimu	Muka	Muli
He/She	Uwe	Naa	Aka	Ali
They	Ubo	Niba	Baka	Bali
It	Ikyo	niki	kika	kiri

Examples

English	Rutooro
Go	Genda
Work	Kora
Come back	Garuka
Read	Soma

Read on the next pages the various tenses of these verbs

Present				
nikigenda	Nibagenda	Naagenda	Nimugenda	Nogenda
nikikora	Nibakora	Naakora	Nimukora	Nokora
nikigaruka	Nibagaruka	Naagaruka	Nimugaruka	Nogaruka
nikisoma	Nibasoma	Naasoma	Nimusoma	Nosoma

Yega Orutooro

Past							
Genda	nkagenda	tukagenda	okagenda	mukagenda	akagenda	bakagenda	kikagenda
Kora	nkakora	tukakora	okakora	mukakora	akakora	bakakora	kikakora
Garuka	nkagaruka	tukagaruka	okagaruka	mukagaruka	akagaruka	bakagaruka	kikagaruka
Soma	nkasoma	tukasoma	okasoma	mukasoma	akasoma	bakasoma	kikasoma

Future Simple

	ndigenda	tuligenda	oligenda	muligenda	aligenda	baligenda	kirigenda
Genda	ndigenda	tuligenda	oligenda	muligenda	aligenda	baligenda	kirigenda
Kora	ndikora	tulikora	olikora	mulikora	alikora	balikora	kirikora
Garuka	ndigaruka	tuligaruka	oligaruka	muligaruka	aligaruka	baligaruka	kirigaruka
Soma	ndisoma	tulisoma	olisoma	mulisoma	alisoma	balisoma	kirisoma

Counting

Counting in Rutooro follows a decimal system. Each number from one to ten has a unique word. After ten the word projects the sense that eleven is Ten and One. Nineteen is Ten and Nine. Twenty three is two Tens and three. Sixty seven is Sixty and Seven.

From Twenty to Fifty each decade is presented as a multiple of Ten. Twenty is two tens, Thirty is three tens, Forty is four tens and Fifty is five tens. Each decade from sixty to one hundred adopts unique words related to the numbers six to ten. Batooro like to simply and sometimes to take short cuts if it means less work. This applies in counting as well. Example: Twenty Six is supposed to be " Makumi Abiri na Mukaaga; 2 tens and six".

In practical usage it is Abiri na mukaaga – Makumi (decade) is implied. 237 would be "Bikumi bibiri na makumi asatu na musanju" but in everyday Rutooro 237 is simply "Bibiri asatu na musanju". The hundred and the ten is implied.

Something many younger Batooro may not know is we have a sign language to count to ten using fingers on one hand.

1	Emu
2	Ebiri
3	Isatu
4	Ina
5	Itano
6	Mukaga
7	Musanju
8	munana
9	Mwenda
10	Ikumi
11	Ikumi nemu
12	Ikumi naibiri
13	Ikumi naisatu
14	Ikumi naina
15	Ikumi naitano
16	Ikumi namukaga
17	Ikumi namusanju
18	Ikumi namunana
19	Ikumi namwenda
20	Abiri
21	Abiri neemu
22	Abiri nabiri
23	Abiri naisatu

24	Abiri naina
25	Abiri naitano
26	Abiri namukaga
27	Abiri namusanju
28	Abiri namunana
29	Abiri namwenda
30	Asatu
31	Asatu naemu
32	Asatu na ebiri
33	Asatu na isatu
34	Asatu naina
35	Asatu naitano
36	Asatu namukaga
37	Asatu namusanju
38	Asatu na munana
39	Asatu namwenda
40	Ana
41	Ana naemu
42	Ana naebiri
43	Ana naisatu
44	Ana naina
45	Ana naitano
46	Ana namukaga

47	Ana namusanju
48	Ana namunana
49	Ana namwenda
50	Atano
51	Atano naemu
52	Atano naebiri
53	Atano naisatu
54	Atano naina
55	Atano naitano
56	Atano namukaga
57	Atano namusangu
58	Atano namunana
59	Atano namwenda
60	Nkaga
61	Nkaga nemu
62	Nkaga naibiri
63	Nkaga naisatu
64	Nkaga naina
65	Nkaga naitano
66	Nkaga namukaga
67	Nkaga namusanju
68	Nkaga namunana
69	Nkaga namwenda

70	Nsanju
71	Nsanju naemu
72	Nsanju naebiri
73	Nsanju naisatu
74	Nsanju naina
75	Nsanju naitano
76	Nsanju namukaga
77	Nsanju namusanju
78	Nsanju namunana
79	Nsanju namwenda
80	Kinaana
81	Kinana naemu
82	Kinana naebiri
83	Kinana naisatu
84	Kinana naina
85	Kinana naitano
86	Kinana namukaga
87	Kinana namusanju
88	Kinana namunana
89	Kinana namwenda
90	Kyenda

91	Kyenda naemu
92	Kyenda naibiri
93	Kyenda naisatu
94	Kyenda naina
95	Kyenda na naitano
96	Kyenda na mukaaga
97	Kyenda na musanjju
98	Kyenda na munana
99	Kyenda na mwenda
100	Kikumi
1000	Rukumi
10000	Omutwaro Gumu
100,000	Emitwaro Ikumu
1000000	Akakairu Kamu
1000000000	Akasirira Kamu

Colours

Erangi

Bururu  Blue

Kasagama  Red

Kyenju  Yellow

Kikara  Black

Kirukwera  White

Kanyali  Grey

Kibabi  Green

Kahuukya  Purple

Kitaka  Brown

Yega Orutooro

Days and Months

Ebiro n'emyezi

Julian Businge & Tracy Guma

Days of the Week
Ebiro bya Wiiki

Monday – Balaza

Tuesday – Kyakabiri

Wednesday- Kyakasatu

Thursday – Kyakana

Friday – Kyakatano

Saturday – Kyamukaaga

Sunday – Sabiiti

Months of the Year
Emyezi y'omwaka

January: Okw'okubanza

February: Okwakabiri

March: Okwakasatu

April : Okwakana

May: Okwakataano

June: Okwamukaaga

July: Okwamusanju

August: Okwamunaana

September: Okwamwenda

October: Okwaikumi

November: Okwaikuminakumu

December: Okwaikuminabiri

Julian Businge & Tracy Guma

School

Isomero

Things and people we find in a school
Ebintu n'abantu tusanga mwisomero

Ebyombeko  Buildings

Abegesa
Abasomesa  Teachers

Abacumbi  Cooks

Abeegi
Abasomi  Pupils
Learners

Ebitebe  Classroom

Inoni  Chalk

Bayiro 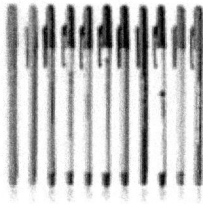 Pen

Yunifomu  Uniform

Yega Orutooro

Erangi   Colours

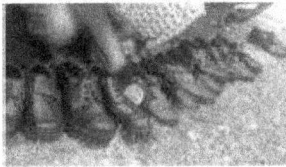

Enkaito   Shoes

Basi yisomero   School Bus

Ekizaniro   Play ground

Kuzaana  Playing

Bwino  Ink

Ebitabu  Books

Parts of the Body

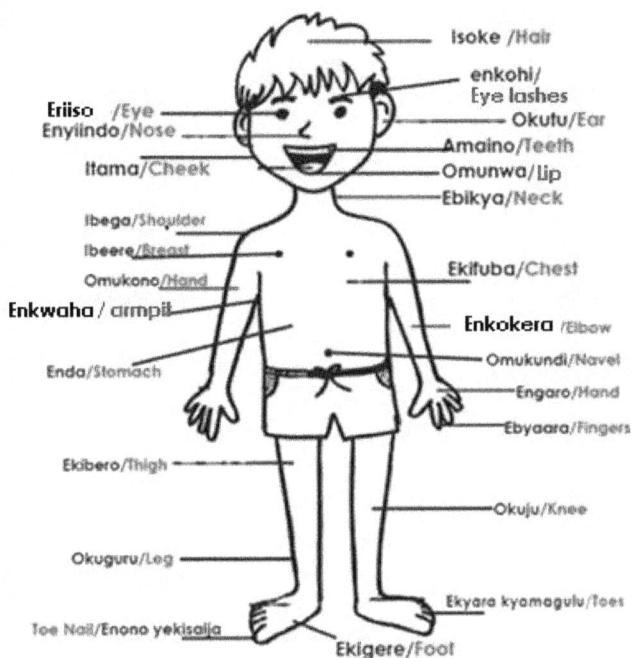

Isoke /Hair

enkohi/
Eye lashes

Eriiso /Eye

Enyiindo/Nose

Okutu/Ear

Amaino/Teeth

Itama/Cheek

Omunwa/Lip

Ebikya/Neck

Ibega/Shoulder

Ibeere/Breast

Omukono/Hand

Ekifuba/Chest

Enkwaha / armpit

Enkokera /Elbow

Enda/Stomach

Omukundi/Navel

Engaro/Hand

Ebyaara/Fingers

Ekibero/Thigh

Okuju/Knee

Okuguru/Leg

Ekyara kyamagulu/Toes

Toe Nail/Enono yekisalja

Ekigere/Foot

Eyebrow: Ekisigi
Eye lashes: Enkohi

Ebicweka by'omubiri

101

Julian Businge & Tracy Guma

Internal Body Parts

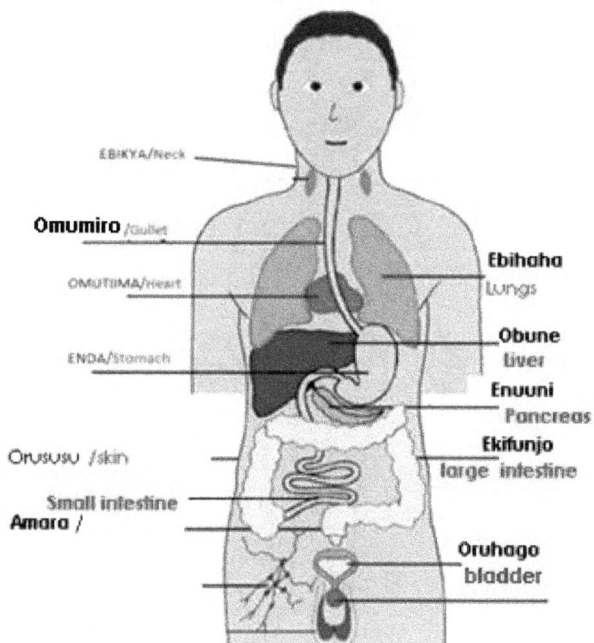

EBIKYA/Neck

Omumiro /Gullet

OMUTIMA/Heart

ENDA/Stomach

Orususu /skin

Small intestine
Amara /

Ebihaha
Lungs

Obune
liver

Enuuni
Pancreas

Ekifunjo
large intestine

Oruhago
bladder

Ebicweka by'omunda

Important Phrases

Beads are worn.

Ekwanzi bazijwara

Tie your shoe laces

**Siba obuguha
bw'ekaito zawe.**

Put on high heeled
shoes.

**Jwara ekaito za
kakondo.**

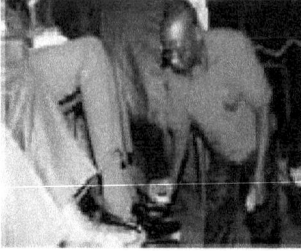

Polish your shoes.

Tera enkaito zawe omubazi.

Reading glasses

Gaarubindi zo kusoma.

Earrings are won by women.

Obwoma bwa matu bujwarwa abakazi.

She is wearing many bracelets.

Ajwaire obukomo bwingi.

Bring a brush and comb your hair.

Leta ekiti otere isoke lyawe.

A girl is wearing a wrap.

Omwisiki asibire leesu

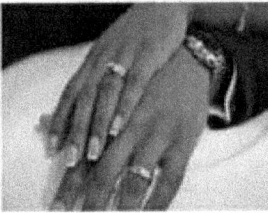

They are wearing wedding rings.

Bajwaire empeta.

Stripped skirt.

Sikaati yo burambi.

Bring your warm jacket.

Leta ekoti yawe ekutagata.

A head scarf

Akatambaara akahamutwe

Handkerchief

Akatambaara

Kwera is putting on a dress.

Kwera ajwaire ekiteeteeyi

Iron your shirt.

Gorra esaati yawe

Wear your necktie.

Siba etayi yawe.

Put on a brown belt.

Weesibe omweko gwa kitaka.

Dad is wearing a kanzu.

Taata ajwaire ekanzu

A child is putting on a skirt.

Omwana ajwaire sikati.

Pour tea in a cup.

Teeka caayi mu kikopo.

Dish out food on a plate.

Ihura ebyokulya ha sahani.

Am cooking in a covered saucepan.

Nicumbira musafuliya efundikirwe.

Switch on the light.

Teekaho etaara

Don't stand in the doorway.

Leka kwemerra mumulyago

Baby is using a spoon.

Omwana nalisa ekigiko.

Dice tomatoes with a knife.

Saara enyanya nomuhyo.

Eat your food using a fork.

Lya ebyokulya ne wuuma.

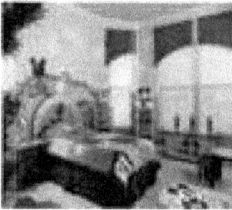

Go and make your bed.

Genda oyale ekitabu kyawe.

Dry the bed sheet on the line.

Oyanike essuuka ha muguha.

Give me the broom

Mpeereza ekisingolezo.

Soap for washing clothes.

Esabuni eyokwogya engoye.

Go in bath-tub and bath.

Genda mu bbafu oyoge.

Sit on the chair.

Ikarra ha ntebe

Bring my tooth-brush.

Leeta brushi yange ya maino.

Set the dining table.

Tekaniza emenza yebyokulya.

Raise your hands.

Imukya emikono haiguru.

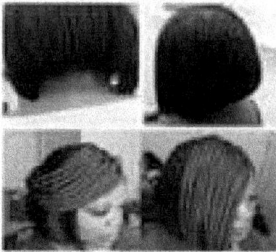

They are braiding her hair.

Nibamusiba isoke lye miguha

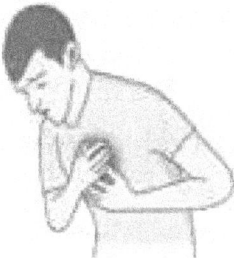

I have chest pain.

Ninsasa ekifuba.

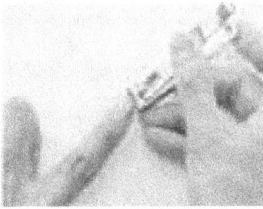

Come let me cut your nails.

Ija nkusale enono.

I have a hand fracture.

Omukono guhendekere

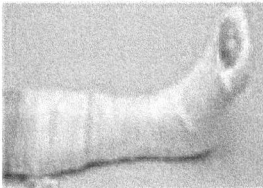

My leg is broken.

Okuguru kucwekere.

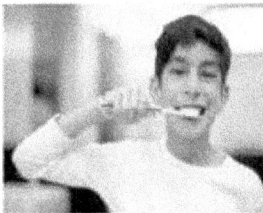

Brush your teeth before you sleep.

Singa amaino otakabyamire

The baby is breast feeding.
Omwana nayonka ibere

113

Go wash your hands.

Genda onabe engaro.

The bride is smart.

Omugole omukazi asemire

Mummy is cooking for us food.

Mau natucumbira ebyokulya.

Yega Orutooro

Put on the kettle
Tekaho ebbinika

Open the window in the morning
Kingura idirisa nyekyakara

Shut the window in the evening
Kinga idirisa rwebagyo

Lock the door with a key
Siba orwigi n'ekisumuruzo

Cover yourself with a blanket
Wesweke bulangiti

Laundry soap
Esabuni yokwogya engoye

Pass me a towel
Mpeereza etawulo

Go and use the toilet
Genda okozese kabunyojo

Scrub yourself with a sponge
Wekute ne kizizo /ekijumankuba

Bring my tooth-brush
Ndetera omuswaki gwange

Make a phone call to your Mum
Terra maama wawe esimu

Mum is shaping her eye-brow
Maama namwa ekisigi

My dad is shaving his beard
Taata namwa omuleju

I have a belly ache
Nindumwa enda, ninsaasa enda

Please scratch my back
Caali nyagura omugongo

Brush your teeth before you sleep
Singa amaino otakabyamire

I have an ear ache
Okutunikunduma –
nindumwa okutu

I have a spot on my chin
Nyina ibara hakaleju

Yega Orutooro

A boy and a girl are walking

Omwojo no mwisiki nibarubata

Go and wash your eyes

Genda onabe amaiso

The bride is smart

Omugole asemire

The groom is naughty

Omugole omusaija muhoole

Daddy doesn't like dirty people

Taata tagonza bantu barofu

We go to school from Monday to Friday

Tugenda haisomero kuruga
Balaza kuhika Kyakataano

Go and ask him what he is going to eat

Genda omukaguze eki
arukugenda kulya

You are lost, where have you been?

Kobuzire, otaha nkaha

Let us go and see our friend in hospital?

Tugende turole munywani waitu
mwirwarro

It's been raining since morning
Kwiha nyekyakara enjura negwa

Don't take alcohol before eating anything
Otanywa amaarwa otakaliire kantu

**Children below 18 years are not
supposed to drink beer**
Abana hansi ye'myaka ikumi na
munaana tibasemerire kunywa
amaarwa

**Yesterday they stole my phone and I
don't have money to buy a new one.**
Ijo baibirege esimu yange kandi
tinyine sente zokugura endi

**You are a man and you say you don't
have money, go look for a job**
Oli musaijja ngu toina sente,
genda oserre omulimo

Before you sleep kneel down and pray
Otakabyamire, banza oteze amaju
osabe

Yega Orutooro

My sister wants a new dress for
Christmas
> Owanyina nyowe nagonza orugoye
> rwa kiro kikuru ruhyaka

The health worker told me to sleep under a
mosquito net everyday
> Ow'ebyobwomezi akangamba
> mbyamege mukatimba kemibu

I was given work to translate these
words from English to Rutooro.
> Nkahebwa omulimo gw'okuhindura
> ebigambo kubiiha murujungu kubita
> murutooro

I started on Monday to do this work
> Gunu omulimo nkagutandika
> balaza

I grew up knowing I have to respect my
parents
> Nkakura nimanya nyina kuha
> abazaire bange ekitinisa

It's not good to be jealous of your friend
> Tikiri kirungi kugirra munywani
> wawe ihali.

Let's trust each other and love one another
Leka twesigengana kandi tugonze ngana.

Mistakes are made by human beings
Ensobi zikorwa abantu

We get many things from outside countries like; phones, cars, radios, iron etc.
Twiha ebintu bingi munsizaheru; nka motoka, esiimu, rediyo, nebindi bingi

The children are playing football
Abaana nibazaana omupiira

We say prayers everyday
Tusaba buli kiro

Yega Orutooro

Ngoza kusoma

Tandika

Webale muno

Oraale kurungi

Yega Orutooro

Professions

Obukugu

Omulinzi
w'obusinge

Police
Officer

Omukuru mu
byokwombeka

Engineer

Omuramuzi

Judge

Magistrate

Omuzalisa

Midwife

Omwegesa
Omusomesa  Teacher

Omusirikale  Soldier

Omufumu  Doctor

Omubaizi  Carpenter

Omuheesi  Blacksmith

Omwombeki  Builder

Hospital

Irwarro
Sipatara

The hospital is the place where we go to get treatment when we are sick.
Obuturwara, batujanjabira mwirwarro

Doctors (they treat patients and perform operations and surgeries)
Abafumu (bajanjaba kandi basemeza abarwaire)

Dentist (a doctor for treatment of teeth related issues and diseases)
Abafumu bamaino batujanjaba endwaire zamaino

Midwives help pregnant mothers give birth.
Abazalisa bakonyera mukuzalisa abakyara

Patients	-	Abarwaire
Drugs	-	Emibazi
Injection	-	Enkinzo
Operate	-	Kusemeza
Pregnant Woman	-	Omukazi aine enda
People	-	Abantu
Diseases	-	Endwaire
To have diarrhea	-	Kuturuka/kucugura
Diarrhea	-	Encugura, ensese
Fever	-	Omuswija
Vomiting	-	Entanaka
Cough	-	Enkorro
Nose Cold	-	Ekihinzi
Headache	-	Omutwe
Stomachache	-	Kurumwa munda

Julian Businge & Tracy Guma

Religion

Ediini

ESAARA YAMUKAMA WAITU	OUR FATHER PRAYER
Isitwe ali omwiguru, Ibara lyawelyezibwe, Obukama bwawe bwije ebogonza bikorwe omunsi, nkwoku bikorwa omwiguru, Otuhe ebyokulya byaitu ebyahati. Otuganyire ebyokusisa byaitu nkaitwe okutuganyira abatusisira, Otatuleka tukohebwa baitu otuune omububi, obukama nobusobozi ,nekitinisa byawe ebiiro nebiiro. Amiina	Our Father, who art in heaven, Hallowed be your Name, Your Kingdom come, Yours will be done in earth, As it is in heaven. Give us this day our daily bread. And forgive us our trespasses, As we forgive them that trespass against us. And lead us not into temptation, But deliver us from evil. For thine is the kingdom, The power, and the glory, For ever and ever. Amen.

EMBABAZI	THE GRACE
Embabazi za Mukama waitu Yesu Kristo, nokugonza okwa Ruhanga, nokuterana okwomwoyo ogurukwera, biikale naitwe itweno ebiro nebiro Amiina.	May the grace of our Lord Jesus Christ, and the love of God, and the fellowship of the Holy Spirit be with us all, now and evermore. Amen.

Worship	-	**Kuhaisaniza**
Praise	-	**Kukugiza**
He saves	-	**Ajuna**
He reigns	-	**Alema**
Hope	-	**Kunihira**
Give thanks	-	**Kusima**
Faith	-	**Kwikiriza**

Yega Orutooro

Holy Bible

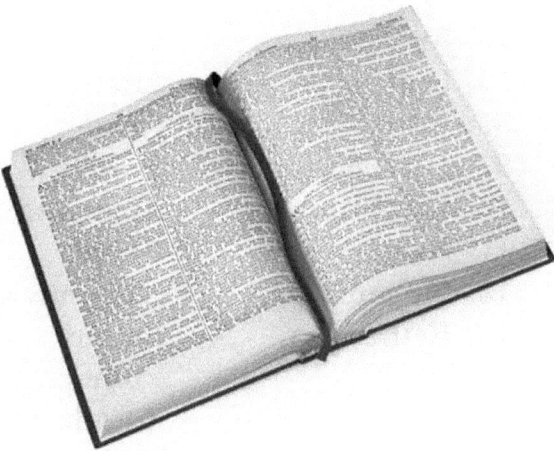

Ekitabu Ekirukwera

133

Old Testament
Endagano Enkuru

1. Genesis - Okubanza
2. Exodus - Okuruga
3. Leviticus - Abalevi
4. Numbers - Okubara
5. Deuteronomy - Ekyebiragiro
6. Joshua - Yosuha
7. Judges - Abaramuzi
8. Ruth - Rusi
9. 1 & 2 Samuel - Samwiri
10. 1 & 2 Kings - Abakama
11. Ezra - Ezira
12. Nehemiah - Nehemiya
13. Esther - Esiteri
14. Job - Yobu
15. Psalms - Zabuli
16. Proverbs - Enfumo
17. Ecclesiastes
18. Song of Solomon- Ebizina bya Sulumani Empami
19. Isaiah - Isaya
20. Jeremiah - Yeremiya
21. Lamentations - Empamo
22. Ezekiel - Ezekeri
23. Daniel - Daneri

24. Hosea   -   Yosiya
25. Joel   -   Yoweri
26. Amos   -   Amosi
27. Obadiah -   Obadiya
28. Jonah   -   Yona
29. Micah   -   Mika
30. Nahum   -   Nahamu
31. Habakkuk -   Habakuku
32. Zephaniah-   Zefaniya
33. Haggai   -   Haggai
34. Zachariah -   Zakaliya
35. Malachi -   Maraki

New Testament
Endagano Empyaka

1.	Matthew	-	Matayo
2.	Mark	-	Maliko
3.	Luke	-	Luka
4.	John	-	Yohana
5.	Acts	-	Ebikorwa by'akwenda
6.	Romans	-	Abarumi
7.	1 Corinthians	-	1 Abakolinso
8.	2 Corinthians	-	2 Abakolinso
9.	Galatians	-	Abagaratiya
10.	Ephesians	-	Abefeso
11.	Philippians	-	Abafiripu
12.	Colossians	-	Abakilisayo
13.	Thessalonians	-	Abatesolonika

Yega Orutooro

Nature

Julian Businge & Tracy Guma

Animals

Ebisoro

Yega Orutooro

Ente

Cow

Embuzi

Goat

Entaama

Sheep

Enjaangu

Cat

Empunu

Pig

Wakame

Rabbit

Embwa

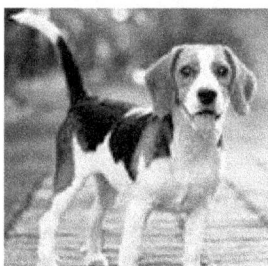

Dog

Birds
Enyonyi

Enkoko   Hen

Ekihungu   Eagle

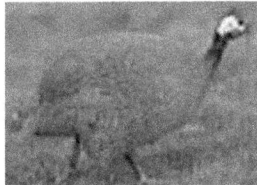

Entajumba   Guinea
                         Fowl

Eriba  Dove

Entuha  Crested crane

Ekiregeya  Weaver bird

Kasuku  Parrot

Yega Orutooro

Endingizi   Owl

Enyange   Egret

Kalore   Marabou stock

Insects
Ebihuka

Enwa

Enwa zimutire

Wasp

He has
been stung
by wasps

Ekijuju
Ebijuju
bituhahire

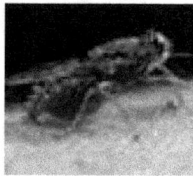

Tsetse fly

We are
infested by
tsetse flies

Ensenene
Ensenene
zigwire

Grasshoppers

The
grasshoppers
are falling

Ekijerre

Ekijerre
kyeserekere
mubinyansi

Cricket

The cricket
is hiding in
grass

Ensohera	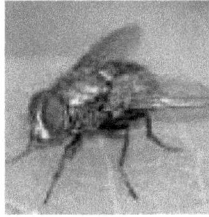	House fly
Ensohera egwire mu mata		The house fly fell in milk
Enyenje		Cockroach
Enyenje irukiire mu kabada		The cockroach has ran into the cupboard
Ekisuzi	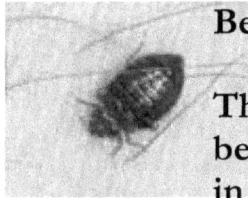	Bedbug
Ekisuzi kiri mu kitabu		The bedbug is in the bed
Enkubebe		Termite
Enkubebe zikara nenswa		Termites stay with white ants.

Enyamumbubi

Enyamumbubi
eyombekere
mu rwigi

Spider

The spider
has built its
web in the
door.

Enkukuni

Enkukuni eri
mumbwa

Flea

The flea is
in the dog

Omubu

Omubu
gundire

Mosquito

I have been
bitten by a
mosquito

Yega Orutooro

Planets

Ebintu by'ensi n'iguru

Izooba		Sun
Okwezi		Moon
Enyunyuzi		Stars
Iguru		Sky
Ensi		Earth

Farming

Seasons	-	Obwire
Rainy season	-	Obwire bwe'njura/ Itumba
Windy season	-	Obwire bwomuyaga/ Kasambura
Dry Season	-	Obwire bw'ekyanda/ Machete

Enfuka  Hoe

Ekipanga  Panga

Endemu  Axe

Enaijoro 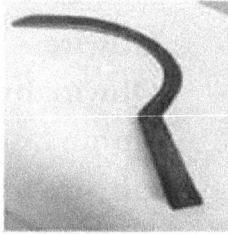 Sickle

Omuhyo Knife

Irisizo  Pasture

Ebisoro  Animals

Ebinyonyi  Birds

Yega Orutooro

Ebihuka — Insects

Kwombera — Weeding

Kutemerra — Pruning

Kugesa — Harvesting

Egaali — Bicycle

Ebirimwa — Plants

Ekisaka — Bush

Ekibira — Forest

Ekigega — Basket

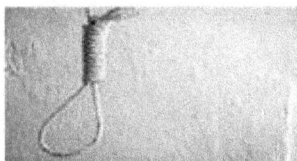

Omuguha — Rope

Yega Orutooro

Bombo   Sprayer

Butusi   Boots

Cash Crops
Ebirimwa

Coffee
Omwani

From coffee we get
instant coffee.
Omumwani
twihamu kawa

Cotton
Pamba

We get the clothes we
wear from cotton
Engoye ezitujwara
tuziha mu pamba

Tobacco
Etaaba

Cigarrettes have
tobacco in them
Sigara ekorwa
kuruga mu taaba

154

Tea
Amajani

We grow tea in Tooro
Tulima amajani mu
Tooro

Cocoa
Koko

Cocoa is grown in
Bundibugyo
Koko erimwa
Bundibugyo

Verbs

A person	Omuntu
Walks	Alibata
To walk	Kulibata
Runs	Airuka
To run	Kwiruka
Ambles	Asenjura
To amble	Kusenjura
Foot	Ekigere
Step	Orutambu
Goes	Agenda
To go	Kugenda
Comes	Aija
To come	Kwija
To come back, to return	Kugaruka
Come back	Garuka

Yega Orutooro

Bicycle	Egaali
To ride a bicycle	Kutemba egaali
To carry a person	Kuheeka omutu
Saddle	Entebbe
Carrier	Kaliya
Peddles	Ebigere
Breaks	Ebiziiza
To break	Kusiba
Tyre/s	Omu /emi piira
Handle bars	Amahembe
Go fast	Kwiruka
Rims	Orupanga

Car	Motoka
Drive	Vuga
To drive	Kuvuga
Driver	Dereva
Overtake	Kuhingura / Kurabaho
To stop	Kwemerra
Steering wheel	Steringi
Klaxon	Engombe
To hoot , honk	Kuteera engombe
Wheel	Enziga
Tyres	Emipiira

Yega Orutooro

Motor cycle	Pikipiki
Exhaust pipe	Omujuba
Exhaust pipes	Emijuba
To break	Kusiba
Aircraft	Enyonyi
A boat	Eryato
A ship	Emeeri , eryato

Foreign Words

A list of words currently accepted as Rutooro but originating in other languages. Invariably if a thing did not exist the Batooro adopted the name from the language of introduction. In some cases some creative person coined a Rutooro word e.g. kainamira = intravenous drip! Research is continuing to find words in contemporary Rutooro which can be identified as assimilated from other languages.

Rutooro	English	Origin
Avuna	Oven	English
Barozi	Governor	Balozi (Swa) - Ambassador
Biralifuru	Bloody fool	English
Booliingo	intense love	Lingala

Buluji	Bugle	English
Busiki	Whisky	English
Cediro	Cidar	English
Diisi	DC (district commissioner	English
Dimeni	Supervisor	English, headman
Ebendera	Flag	Spanish, bandera
Ekoti	Jacket, coat	English
Enkwanzi	Beads	Arabic, Alkharz
Esaati	Shirt	English

Esapuli	Rosary	Sabili Arabic
Esirwali	Trousers	Shalwar, Silwar (Urdu, Punjabi)
Fuleera	Religious brother	Frère (French)
Furampeni	Frying pan	English
Garubindi	Reading glasses	Swahili, Darubini, Microscope
Jokoni	Kitchen	Swahili, (Jikoni)
Kabana	Governor	
Kaikoti	High court	English
Kalifomu	Chloroform	English

Kalituusi	Eucalyptus	English
Kapulisasi	Cypress	English
Keleziya	Catholic church	Eclesias (Spanish)
Kitabu	Book	Swahili, Arabic (kitab)
Kizibiti	Exhibit	English
Kubatiza	Baptize	English
Makatara	Contract	?
Medikoro	Medical	English
Meza	Table	Spa, port: Messa
misani	Mission	English

Mpisi	Cook	Swahili, mpishi, pika=cook
Mu ndaani	In the mine	Swahili - ndani, inside
Omudaali	Medal	English
Omulefu	Trousers	Swahili, mrefu long
Omupadiri	Father (priest)	Padre (Spanish)
Pere	Father (priest)	French, Père
Piida	PWD	English abbreviation

Piisi	PC (provincial comm .)	English
Potoro	Patrol	English
Ruduvasi	Road supervisor	road overseer
Rupiya	Money	Hindi, English, rupee
Saati	Shirt	English
Samuchi	Sandwitch	English
Sigiri	Charcoal bunner	??
Sipatara	Hospital	English to Hindi aspataal to Rutooro

		spatara
Skaati	Skirt	eng
Spekita	Inspector	
Siyagi	Butter	Swahili

Visit Tooro

- Kibale Forest National Park
- Tooro-Semuliki Reserve
- Crater Lakes such as Saaka and Kigere
- The King's Palace
- The Snow-capped Rwenzori Mountain
- Queen Elizabeth National Park
- Karambi Royal Tombs
- Amabere ga Nyinamwiru
- Semuliki Hot springs

Crater Safari Lodge

View of Rwenzori Mountains

An aerial view of Kyaninga Lodge

Puzzles and Quizzes

	Write the answer in English	
0	Ikumi naitaano	
1	Ikumi naisatu	
2	Musanju	
3	Ikumi	
4	Mweda	
5	Mukaaga	
6	Emu	
7	Ziro	
8	Ikumi nemu	
9	Ibiri	
10	Itaano	

11	Ikumi namweda	
12	makumi Abiri	
13	Ikumi namunaana	
14	Abiri nemu	
15	Ikumi na musanju	
16	Ikumi naibiri	
17	Ikumi naitaano	
18	Ikumi na mu kaaga	
19	Ikumi naina	
20	Ikumi naisaitu	
21	Ikumi nemu	

Write the answer in Rutooro

_____

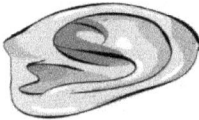

_____

_____

_____

_____

_____

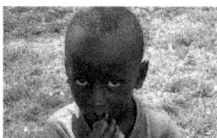

_____

_____

Yega Orutooro

Month _____

Friday _____

Mr/Sir _____

Thursday _____

Hospital _____

Pleased to meet you _____

How are you _____

Match the Words

Girl	Amata
Key	Omupiira
Car	Omukazi
Saturday	Esafuliya
I want	Ndikurungi muno
Monday	Ikumi
I am not well	Enkoko
Ball	Ekisumuruzo
Sauce Pan	Tindi Kurungi
Woman	Mwisiki
Milk	Kyamukaga
I am very well	Motoka
Ten	Balaza
Hen, chicken	Ningonza

Yega Orutooro

Ebintu nabantumwisomero

```
.  .  .  .  .  .  O  T  I  A  K  N  E  S  E  O  H  S  .  .  .  .
P  E  N  B  A  Y  I  R  O  E  B  E  T  N  E  S  K  S  E  D  .  .  U
.  O  H  A  S  N  E  G  A  B  L  O  O  H  C  S  .  .  .  .  .  .  M
.  .  .  .  U  N  I  F  O  R  M  Y  U  N  I  F  O  M  U  .  .  .  A
.  .  .  .  A  N  A  Z  U  K  G  N  I  Y  A  L  P  .  .  .  .  .  L
.  P  U  P  I  L  S  A  B  A  S  O  M  I  .  .  .  .  .  .  .  .  A
.  .  A  N  A  A  B  A  S  L  I  P  U  P  .  .  .  .  .  .  .  .  K
Y  A  R  D  I  R  E  M  B  O  B  O  O  K  S  E  B  I  T  A  B  U  E
.  .  .  .  B  U  I  L  D  I  N  G  S  E  B  Y  O  M  B  E  K  O  L
T  E  A  C  H  E  R  S  A  B  A  S  O  M  E  S  A  .  .  .  .  .  I
.  O  R  E  M  O  S  E  Y  I  S  A  B  S  U  B  L  O  O  H  C  S  C
I  N  K  B  W  I  N  O  C  O  L  O  R  S  E  R  A  N  G  I  .  .  N
.  .  .  O  R  I  N  A  Z  I  K  E  D  N  U  O  R  G  Y  A  L  P  E
C  H  A  L  K  I  N  O  N  I  I  B  M  U  C  U  M  O  K  O  O  C  P
.  .  T  E  A  C  H  E  R  S  A  B  E  G  E  S  A  .  .  .  .  .
C  L  A  S  S  R  O  O  M  S  E  B  I  T  E  B  E  .  .  .  .  .
```

Word directions and start points are formatted: (Direction, X, Y)

BOOKS-EBITABU (E,11,8)
BUILDINGS-EBYOMBEKO (E,5,9)
CHALK-INONI (E,1,14)
CLASSROOMS-EBITEBE (E,1,16)
COLORS-ERANGI (E,9,12)
COOK-OMUCUMBI (W,22,14)
DESKS-ENTEBE (W,20,2)
INK-BWINO (E,1,12)

PEN-BAYIRO (E,1,2)
PENCIL-EKALAMU (N,23,14)
PLAYGROUND-EKIZANIRO (W,22,13)
PLAYING-KUZANA (W,16,5)
PUPILS-ABAANA (W,14,7)
PUPILS-ABASOMI (E,2,6)
SCHOOL BAG-ENSAHO (W,16,3)
SCHOOL BUS-BASIYESOMERO (W,22,11)

SHOES-ENKAITO (W,19,1)
TEACHERS-ABASOMESA (E,1,10)
TEACHERS-ABEGESA (E,3,15)
UNIFORM-YUNIFOMU (E,5,4)
YARD-IREMBO (E,1,8)

Player Name: _____

Ebintu nabantumwisomero

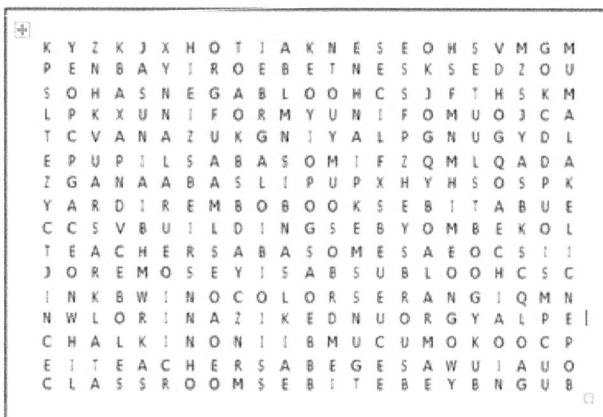

```
K Y Z K J X H O T I A K N E S E O H S V M G M
P E N B A Y I R O E B E T N E S K S E D Z O U
S O H A S N E G A B L O O H C S J F T H S K M
L P K X U N I F O R M Y U N I F O M U O J C A
T C V A N A Z U K G N I Y A L P G N U G Y D L
E P U P I L S A B A S O M I F Z Q M L Q A D A
Z G A N A A B A S L I P U P X H Y H S O S P K
Y A R D I R E M B O B O O K S E B I T A B U E
C C S V B U I L D I N G S E B Y O M B E K O L
T E A C H E R S A B A S O M E S A E O C S I I
J O R E M O S E Y I S A B S U B L O O H C S C
I N K B W I N O C O L O R S E R A N G I Q M N
N W L O R I N A Z I K E D N U O R G Y A L P E
C H A L K I N O N I I B M U C U M O K O O C P
E I T E A C H E R S A B E G E S A W U I A U O
C L A S S R O O M S E B I T E B E Y B N G U B
```

Find the following words in the puzzle. (Both, English and Rutooro).
Words are hidden ↑ ↓ → ← and ↘ .

BOOKS-EBITABU
BUILDINGS-EBYOMBEKO
CHALK-INONI
CLASSROOMS-EBITEBE
COLORS-ERANGI
COOK-OMUCUMBI
DESKS-ENTEBE
INK-BWINO

PEN-BAYIRO
PENCIL-EKALAMU
PLAY GROUND-EKIZANIRO
PLAYING-KUZANA
PUPILS-ABAANA
PUPILS-ABASOMI
SCHOOL BAG-ENSAHO
SCHOOL BUS-BASI YESOMERO

SHOES-ENKAITO
TEACHERS-ABASOMESA
TEACHERS-ABEGESA
UNIFORM-YUNIFOMU
YARD-IREMBO

Glossary

Academics	Ebyenyegesa
Accident	Butandwa
Afternoon	Nyamusana
Air	Orwoya
All of them	Bona hamu
All of us	Itwena
Angel	Malaika
Attempt	Lengaho
Author	Muhandikiwebitabu
Ball	Mupira
Battle	Orutabaro
Beans	Bihimba
Beard	Omuleju
Black and white goat	Kitanga
Black goat	Kibogo
Blood	Esagama
Boast	Kwepanka/ Kwehemba
Boat	Eryato
Body order	Ekikara
Bold head	Oruhara
Bore hole	Mulikonda
Bottle	Cuupa
Breath	Kwikya
Breath	Kwikya
Bull	Numi

Clan	Ruganda
Clap your hands	Tera engaro
Classroom	Ekitebe
Cold	(weather)
Cold	(item)Embeho
Cry	Kurra
Dad	Taata
Darkness	Omwirima
Dawn	Orukyakya
Day before	Ijweri
Dead of night	Itumbi
Death	Ruufu
Dining	Iriiro
Doll	Dole
Dream	Ekirooto
Dusk	Akairirizi
Eat	Kulya
Elderly	Mukuru
Electricity	Amasanyarazi
Energy	Endasi
Fees	Empeera, omusaara
Feet cracks	Enkyakya
Female chicken	Nyonge
Female cow	Nyana
Female dog	Mbwakati
Female goat	Ruusi
Fight	Rwana
Fire	Muurro

Fool	Mudoma
Friends	Enganjani/abanywani
Games	Emizano
Germinate	Kumera
Ghost	Omuzimu
Goat	Mbuzi
Grandkids	Baijukuru
Grey hair	Enju
Grinding stone	Rubengo
Hail stone	Orubaale
Happiness	Kusemererwa
Hatred	Enobi
Heap	Entuumo
Heart	Omutima
Heat	Ekirro
Hen, chicken	Nkoko
Hospital	Irwarro, sipatara
Hours	Esaha
Illness	Burwaire
Instruct	Kuragira
Iron sheet	Amabati
Kneel	Teza amaju
Laugh	Seka
Lie on back	Garama
Lie on stomach	Kwejumika
Life	Obwomeezi
Light	Ekyererezi
Lion	Ntale

Marriage	Obuswere, obuswezi
Mat	Omukeka
Minutes	Edakika
Money	Sente/ensimbi rupiya
Moon	Mweezi/kweezi
Morning	Nyenkyakara
Mountain	Rusozi
Mummy	Mama
Net	Akatimba
Night	Ekiro
No	Nangwa
Old man	Mugurusi
Palm	Ekiganja
Paper	Orupapura
Papers	Empapura
Party	Obugenyi
Pastors	Baahule, baliisa
Pet name	Empaako
Phone	Esimu
Pimple	Embarabi
Plants	Ebimera
Pot	Ensoha
Party (political)	Ekitebe
Rainbow	Omuhangaizima
Read	Soma
Religion	Edini
Remember	Ijuka
Rope	Muguha

Rubbish	Ebisasiro
Sack	Ensahu
Sadness	Obujune
Safety pin	Ekikwaso
Seconds	Edakika
Shade	Ekiituuru
Sheep	Entaama
Shout	Toka
Sickness	Burwaire
Sit	Ikarra
Skin	Omubiri
Sleep	Byama
Smell	Nunka
Sneeze, to	Semura , kwe
Snow	Ebirika
Spots	Obugondo
Squat	Sitama
Stones	Amabaale
Strength	Amaani
Stub	Cumita
Sweep	Singorra
Tail	Mukira
Teach	Yegesa
Teacher	Mwegesa
Teacher, catechist	Musomesa
Thorns	Amahwa
Time	Obwire
Today	Kirokinu, hati

Tomorrow	Nyenkya
Totem	Omuziro
Trade	Obusubuzi
Tree	Muti
Tribe	Ihanga
War	Rutaro
Watch	Saha
Wound	Kihoya

Meet the Authors

Tracy Norah Guma

Tracy is born in Fort Portal town, Western Uganda and was raised up in a distinctive Tooro Home where speaking the Rutooro language dominated her upbringing.

Tracy received her primary and secondary school education in Fort Portal. She grew up in a very close-knit family where community spirit and friendships were considered as the main support structures for young people. These core values helped Tracy to create lasting friendships, develop an enduring bond with Tooro and many fond memories.

Following completion of her Secondary education in Uganda, Tracy continued with her studies in the United Kingdom, where she obtained a BA Honour in Business Studies and accounting at South Bank University, London. Since her graduation, Tracy has worked as a Civil Servant in various grades at key UK Government Departments.

Tracy is happily married to Guma Komwiswa, and they have 4 children together; Pearl, Holly, Trisha and Zyon to whom she dedicates this book as part of their upbringing, and early learning of the fundamentals of Tooro culture and language.

Tracy's motivation and enthusiasm for co-authoring this book was driven by her love for Tooro as her birthplace, which offers a very rich language, heritage and culture not found anywhere else.

Tracy herself is a fluent Rutooro speaker and would encourage fellow Batooro and all those interested in learning basic aspects of the language to utilize this publication as an opportunity to get started. For more information email: adyeritracy@yahoo.com

Julian Businge

She is a Mutooro born and raised in Uganda. A mubiito by clan. She came to the UK to join her husband and start their family .She is an Award winning motivational speaker, Author of Increase Your Cash Flow: Serviced Accommodation, Breakthrough Declarations of a praying wife and has co-authored many other books. She is a property and business coach, hosts live property workshops .More than anything she is a child of God, happily married to Dr Patrick Businge and together have two children. She is passionate about teaching the Rutooro culture. For more information visit www.julianbusinge.com or email her at info@julianbusinge.com